SARAH TIMM

2023-2024 Nashville Travel Guide

Top Attractions, Restaurants, Hikes & Activities to Explore in the Nashville Area

Copyright © 2023 by Sarah Timm

All rights reserved. No part of this publication may be reproduced, stored or transmitted in any form or by any means, electronic, mechanical, photocopying, recording, scanning, or otherwise without written permission from the publisher. It is illegal to copy this book, post it to a website, or distribute it by any other means without permission.

Sarah Timm asserts the moral right to be identified as the author of this work.

Sarah Timm has no responsibility for the persistence or accuracy of URLs for external or third-party Internet Websites referred to in this publication and does not guarantee that any content on such Websites is, or will remain, accurate or appropriate.

Designations used by companies to distinguish their products are often claimed as trademarks. All brand names and product names used in this book and on its cover are trade names, service marks, trademarks and registered trademarks of their respective owners. The publishers and the book are not associated with any product or vendor mentioned in this book. None of the companies referenced within the book have endorsed the book.

First edition

This book was professionally typeset on Reedsy.
Find out more at reedsy.com

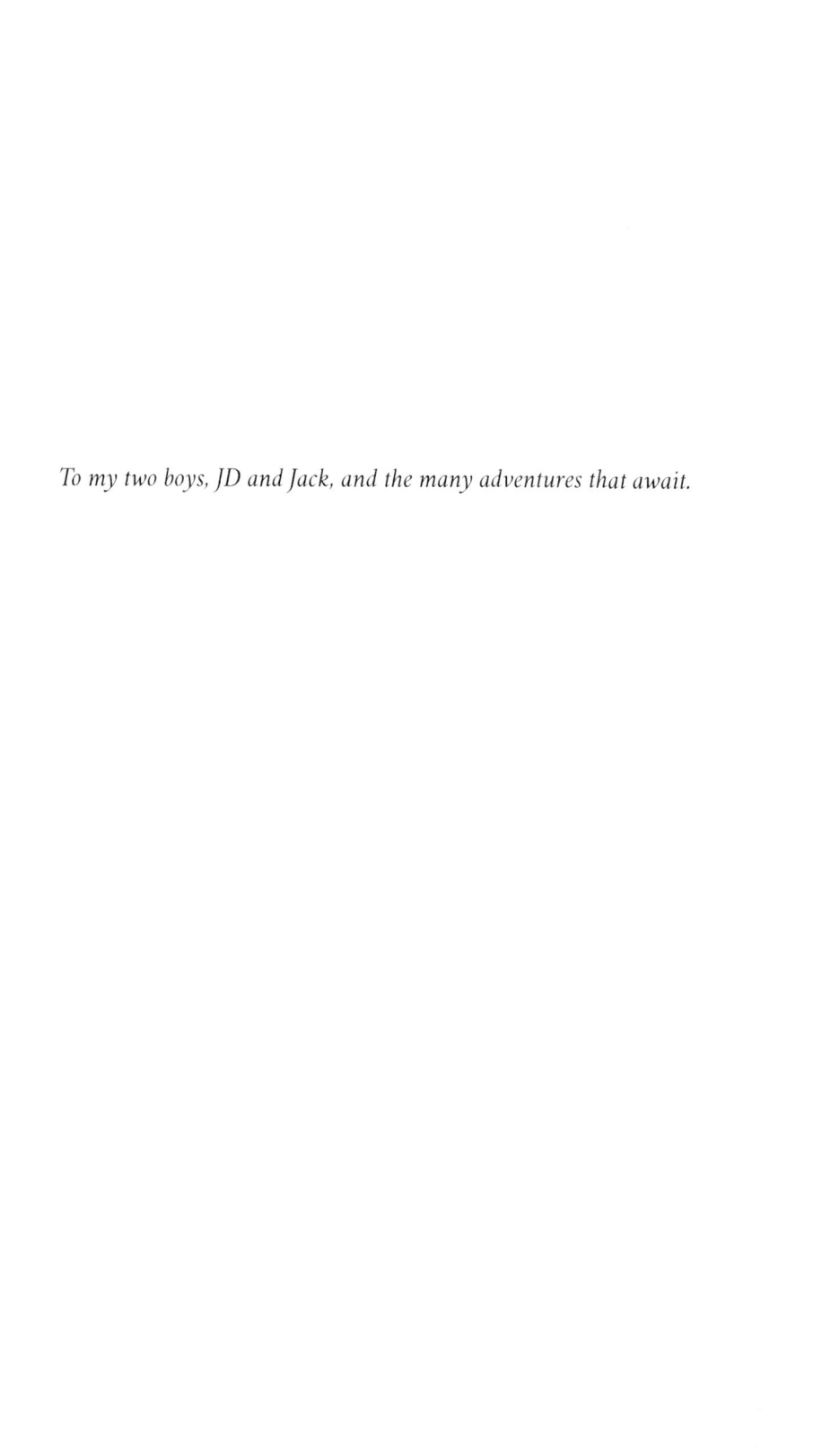

To my two boys, JD and Jack, and the many adventures that await.

"You'll never do a whole lot unless you're brave enough to try."

- DOLLY PARTON

Contents

1 Introduction	1
Welcome to Music City, Y'all!	1
Our History	2
What to Expect	3
2 Pre-Trip Planning	5
Nashville Weather	5
Where to Stay	7
BNA Airport	11
Reservations	12
3 Get Your Bearings	13
Maps	13
Transportation	14
Locally Owned Markets	15
Farmer's Markets	17
4 Live Music	19
Venues	19
Honky Tonks	24
5 Eat	28
Breakfast and Brunch	28
Dinner	33
6 Drink	40
Bars (The Ones that Aren't Honky Tonks)	40
Dives	44
Breweries	47

Vineyards	51
Distilleries	53
7 Sports	57
Football	57
Hockey	58
Baseball	59
Soccer	61
8 Hike	63
State Parks and Waterfalls	63
State and National Forests	67
Lakes	69
9 Bring the Kids	71
Family Activities	71
Parks	74
10 Arts and Theater	77
Broadway Musicals	77
Museums	78
Art Galleries	80
11 Holidays	83
Christmas	83
Christmas Pop-Up Bars	86
Fourth of July	87
12 Conclusion	91
About the Author	93

1

Introduction

Welcome to Music City, Y'all!

I am so excited to be writing this book. With friends and family regularly traveling far and wide to visit Nashville, I am forever sharing tips and favorite spots. I've always half-joked about creating some variety of pamphlet to hand out to visitors but instead decided to bite the bullet and write a little book containing what I believe to be the best of experiences in each category. I plan to print several copies to give to clients, friends, and family, but thought, why not go ahead and share it with the world?

In this guide, you will find many helpful tips for planning your perfect trip to Nashville. Whether you are a music lover, a foodie, an outdoor enthusiast, or a family on vacation, this book has you covered. From the best restaurants to the top live music venues (as well as the lesser-known ones), from scenic waterfall hikes to the most exciting sports events, you will find it all here.

Please bear in mind that this is not intended to be a comprehensive guide, but to inspire you to discover more. Additionally, our city is so alive and ever-changing that I plan to write further editions, enlisting the help of friends, family, and other long-time locals to offer their own favorite spots and insider tips.

Nashville is a place with a rich history, famous not just for its contributions to music, but also arts and culture. It has evolved over time, but its heart remains firmly rooted in its traditions and values. From the iconic Honky Tonks on Broadway to the natural beauty of the adjacent State Parks and waterfalls, Nashville has something for absolutely everyone. I am thrilled to share my own recommendations with you, and can't wait for you to fall in love with this city and its surroundings, just as so many have.

Let's dive in and explore!

Our History

Our growing metropolis may be best known for its incredible music scene, but did you know that Nashville's roots go all the way back to the 1700s when the region was first inhabited by Native American tribes like the Cherokee, Creek, and Shawnee? I'm going to be honest with you, I am slightly embarrassed to say I wasn't familiar with the history prior to sitting down to write this, and I'd certainly be remiss to not include a bit of Nashville history in a book about Nashville.

Fast forward to 1779, when a brave group of pioneers, led by the fearless James Robertson and John Donelson, founded Nashville on the banks

INTRODUCTION

of the Cumberland River. In no time, the city became a hot spot for trade and commerce, shipping goods like tobacco and cotton all over the place. By the mid-1800s, Nashville had become the biggest city in Tennessee.

But things got a little rocky during the Civil War when Union and Confederate forces both recognized Nashville's strategic importance. The city was captured by Union soldiers in 1862 and heavily fortified for military operations. After the war, Nashville bounced back in a big way, becoming a center for music, education, healthcare, and even publishing.

Today, Nashville is a thriving cultural hub, with a rich history just waiting to be explored by visitors of all ages.

So come on down and immerse yourself in the sights, sounds, and stories of Nashville. Whether you're a music lover, a history buff, or just looking for a good time, this city is sure to steal your heart!

What to Expect

Nashville is a city with a unique blend of Southern charm and big-city energy. You can expect to find friendly locals, delicious food, and an endless array of entertainment options. The possibilities are endless, whether you are here for a weekend getaway or a longer vacation.

Expect to be serenaded by live music at every turn, indulge in some of the best food and drinks in the South, and immerse yourself in the city's history and culture. With this guide, I can't promise a stress-free trip, but I sure hope it will take some of the stress of planning off your shoulders. I can promise, however, that it'll be a trip packed with exciting adventures and unforgettable experiences. So, buckle up and get ready to explore like a local.

2

Pre-Trip Planning

Nashville Weather

It's no secret that the South can get pretty hot and humid, and Nashville is no exception. But fear not, because with a bit of preparation, you can make the most of your visit no matter what time of year you're here.

Disclaimer: In a word, Nashville weather is unpredictable. I've been hiking in shorts and a t-shirt the day after Christmas on a sunny 70° day, and have also been bundled up on a windy 40° in April wanting to snuggle up with some hot cocoa in front of the fire. But *very generally* speaking, here's what you can expect:

Let's start with **January**, when you'll typically see some chilly temperatures in the 30s and 40s, with occasional snow or ice.

February is much the same but with a little less snow and a little more rain.

March brings with it the first signs of spring, with average highs in the 60s and lows in the 40s.

April and **May** are some of the most beautiful months in Nashville, with temperatures warming up into the 70s and 80s with the city awash in colorful blooms and greenery.

June through **September** are the warmest months of the year, with highs in the high 80s and oftentimes creeping into the 90s. It can get pretty muggy during this time, so be sure to stay hydrated and take breaks in the shade.

October is a favorite of many locals, with crisp, comfortable temperatures in the 60s and 70s and gorgeous fall foliage.

November brings with it cooler temperatures and the occasional frost, but still plenty of opportunities to enjoy the great outdoors.

December can be chilly with some rare snow, but that adds to the magic of the holiday season and festive events all around town.

No matter when you visit, the city is always buzzing with excitement and endless possibilities. In the spring, you can stroll through the blooming gardens and catch live music on every corner. In the summer, you can cool off with a refreshing drink on a rooftop bar or enjoy outdoor festivals under the warm sun. Even in the winter, Nashville's holiday lights and cozy venues create a magical atmosphere that will warm your heart (see the "Holidays" chapter). No matter the season, Nashville guarantees an adventure.

Where to Stay

Whether you're looking for a luxury hotel or a cozy Airbnb, there are plenty of options to choose from. Here's a quick rundown of Nashville's main neighborhoods and a brief description of each that will hopefully help you find your vibe:

- **Downtown Nashville** buzzes with energy, showcasing the heart of the city's vibrant music scene, iconic honky-tonks, and thriving nightlife.

- **SoBro** (South of Broadway) is one of the main downtown areas. It's a trendy neighborhood with sleek high-rises, hip restaurants, and a lively atmosphere, attracting both locals and visitors alike.

- **The Gulch** is a modern and upscale district, known for its chic boutiques, trendy eateries, and vibrant, Instagram-able urban vibe.

- **East Nashville** is a buzzing and eclectic neighborhood, brimming with artistic flair, offbeat bars, quaint shops, and a flourishing food scene that showcases the area's creative and diverse spirit.

- **Germantown/Jefferson Street** offers a great blend of historic charm and trendy vibes, featuring restored Victorian homes, trendy eateries, and a revitalized Jefferson Street corridor that pays homage to Nashville's rich and diverse heritage.

- **Opryland/Music Valley** is a vibrant entertainment district surrounding the iconic Grand Ole Opry, offering attractions, shopping, and family-friendly entertainment.

- **The Airport/Donelson/Hermitage** area is a convenient hub near Nashville International Airport, with a mix of residential, commercial, and recreational spaces, including parks and the beautiful Percy Priest Lake.

- **8th Avenue/Melrose** is a hip and happening neighborhood, boasting a mix of unique shops, cozy cafes, and trendy restaurants that cater to diverse tastes.

- **Wedgewood/Houston** is an up-and-coming arts district, with converted warehouses housing art galleries, creative studios, and eclectic shops, attracting a lively community of artists and art enthusiasts.

- **Music Row/Demonbreun/Edgehill** is a neighborhood that pulses with the rhythm of Nashville's music industry. It's a vibrant area filled with recording studios, live music venues, and a mix of modern establishments and historic landmarks.

- **West End/Elliston Place** offers an upbeat atmosphere with a mix of college vibes, trendy bars, and eclectic eateries, attracting a diverse crowd of students, locals, and visitors.

- **Midtown/Vanderbilt** is a bustling neighborhood that combines the energy of a college campus with a vibrant nightlife scene. It's home to a variety of restaurants, bars, and live music venues, making it a go-to spot for entertainment and socializing.

- **Sylvan Park** is a charming and laid-back neighborhood with tree-lined streets, local shops, and cozy cafes, creating a warm and welcoming community feel.

- **Green Hills** exudes an upscale and affluent vibe, with its high-end shopping centers, boutiques, and elegant homes. It's a refined neighborhood known for its fashionable residents and a hub for luxury retail and dining.

- **Belmont/Hillsboro** has a distinct college-town atmosphere, with its proximity to Belmont University and a mix of charming homes, student hangouts, and trendy shops and restaurants.

- **12South** is an of-the-moment, trendy neighborhood that blends historic charm with a modern, vibrant atmosphere. It offers a mix of stylish boutiques, unique eateries, and bustling coffee shops, attracting a trendy crowd and serving as a hub for local fashion and creativity.

- **Berry Hill** is a small but flourishing neighborhood known for its concentration of recording studios, music-related businesses, and quirky shops, creating a distinct artsy vibe.

- **The Nations/Charlotte** is an up-and-coming neighborhood undergoing revitalization, with an eclectic mix of local shops, breweries, and fun, unique eateries. It has a creative and community-oriented atmosphere, attracting young professionals and artists.

- **North Nashville** is a culturally rich neighborhood known for its historic architecture, soulful music venues, and strong sense of community, reflecting the city's diverse heritage and fostering a warm and welcoming environment.

Nashville's unique neighborhoods offer a rich tapestry of culture, history, and energetic atmospheres. Whether you choose to stay in the heart of downtown, the trendy districts, or the charming residential areas, you'll find something special to explore. With various transportation options, including public transit, ride-sharing services, and walkability, getting around the city is a breeze, ensuring that your Nashville adventure will be filled with memorable experiences no matter where you choose to stay.

BNA Airport

Get ready for a real southern welcome at Nashville International Airport (BNA). This place is buzzing with energy and music from the moment you step off the plane.

BNA is all about celebrating Nashville's musical heritage, so expect to be serenaded by live performances from local musicians and surrounded by displays featuring famous Nashville artists. And when it comes to food and shopping, you can bet that you'll find plenty of local products, like juicy hot chicken and handcrafted guitars.

Don't worry about getting lost in this airport because it's super easy to navigate, with two main terminals, and the more modern and spacious Concourse C serving as the hub for most airlines. But, even the older terminal has plenty of dining and shopping options to keep you entertained.

If you've got a little extra time before your flight, take advantage of their amenities, like charging stations, free Wi-Fi, or a relaxing massage bar.

When you're ready to explore the city, transportation options from BNA are abundant. You can rent a car, grab a taxi or ride-sharing service, or take public transportation. And, since the airport is just a few miles away from downtown Nashville, you can be singing along to your favorite country tunes on Broadway in no time.

So, get ready for a true Nashville experience, starting from the moment you land at BNA. It's all about Southern hospitality, good vibes, and of course, great music.

Reservations

As you probably know, this city is famous for its southern comfort food, BBQ, and hot chicken, but that's just scratching the surface. With the many out-of-this-world dining options in Nashville, be sure to plan ahead and make a few reservations to plan your day around – think dinner and brunch spots – a couple of weeks before your trip.

Not all places require reservations, but it's a good idea to have a few set up, no matter what time of the week or year you'll be in town (see the "Eat" chapter). Of course, eating out for every meal may not be everyone's cup o' tea, but be sure to treat yourself to at least a few memorable Nashville meals. In addition, check out some of the city's farmer's markets and locally-owned markets for some fresh and delicious ingredients to cook up in your kitchen if you have one where you're staying.

3

Get Your Bearings

Maps

Scan each QR code with your phone camera to open the area you'd like to explore.

Neighborhoods

Downtown

Downtown/Midtown Hotels

Where to Park

Music City Walk of Fame

Opryland/Music Valley/Airport Lodging/Convention

Transportation

Getting around Nashville is easy with no shortage of options to suit every traveler's need and mood by the hour (this list doesn't even include pedal taverns, party buses, party tractors, and the like).

By Foot

Strolling through downtown Nashville is a safe and fantastic way to experience the city's sights, sounds, and flavors. With over 70 miles of sidewalks and the John Seigenthaler Pedestrian Bridge linking downtown to the east bank and Nissan Stadium, walking is undoubtedly a great way to go.

By Car

For those who prefer a quicker ride, Uber and Lyft are readily available all over the city.

If you're wanting to explore beyond the city limits, renting a car is your best bet. And if you're feeling adventurous, why not take a scenic drive to some of the nearby state parks and hiking trails?

By Bike

Brand new electric bikes are now available via relaunched Nashville BCycle. Download the BCycle app to find e-bikes & stations, set up your passes, and checkout e-bikes from wherever you are.

By E-Scooter

Plenty of scooter options here, including Bird, Lime, and Spin. Download the apps ahead of time to be ready to ride and be sure you know the rules for safe and legal riding.

By Bus

If you're looking for a more unique experience, why not try out the Music City Circuit? It's a free bus service that runs throughout downtown and midtown Nashville, stopping at popular destinations like the Country Music Hall of Fame and Museum, Ryman Auditorium, and the Johnny Cash Museum. Plus, it's a great opportunity to jam out to some country music on your way to your next destination.

Locally Owned Markets

If you're looking for some fresh local produce or unique finds, check out these neighborhood markets and grocery stores for a true taste of Music City:

- **The Turnip Truck** - This beloved market has two locations in East Nashville and the Gulch. You'll find a wide variety of organic and local produce, as well as prepared foods, supplements, and household goods.

- **Produce Place** - This Hillsboro Village staple has been around since 1988, offering fresh produce, local meats, and other specialty items like homemade salsas and artisan cheeses.

- **Batch Nashville** - This gourmet market in the Sylvan Park neighborhood features an array of local and regional products, including meats, cheeses, baked goods, and pantry items. They also offer grab-and-go meals and a selection of craft beer and wine.

- **Turnip Green Creative Reuse** - Located in the Wedgewood-Houston neighborhood, this nonprofit offers eco-friendly and repurposed items for your home and garden, as well as a variety of art and craft supplies.

- **Nashville Farmers' Market** - This year-round market in Germantown features a diverse selection of local produce, meats, dairy, and artisanal foods, as well as unique shops and eateries. Check out the outdoor farm sheds for seasonal produce and specialty products.

- **International Market & Restaurant** - This market in the Antioch area offers a vast selection of international foods and ingredients, as well as a popular restaurant serving up authentic dishes from around the world.

No matter which market you choose, you're sure to find some delicious and unique items to take home (or to your Airbnb or hotel) with you. Happy shopping!

Farmer's Markets

Looking for more fresh and locally sourced produce? Nashville's farmer's markets offer a unique opportunity to support local farmers and producers while getting your hands on some of the freshest fruits, vegetables, and artisanal products. Here's a list of some of the top farmer's markets in Nashville:

- **Nashville Farmers Market** - This year-round market is a great place to find a wide variety of fresh produce, meats, cheese, and other artisanal goods.

- **Franklin Farmers Market** - Just a short drive south of Nashville, this market features over 80 vendors and is open on Saturdays from May through October.

- **East Nashville Farmers Market** - Located in the low-key cool neighborhood of East Nashville, this market features fresh produce, locally made crafts, and live music.

- **Richland Park Farmers Market** - Set in the picturesque Richland Park neighborhood, this market is open on Saturdays from May through October and features a diverse range of vendors.

- **Hip Donelson Farmers Market** - This market is located in the Donelson neighborhood and is open on Fridays from May through October. In addition to fresh produce, you can also find live music and food trucks.

- **12South Farmers Market** - This market is located in the trendy 12South neighborhood and is open on Tuesdays from May through October. It features a rotating selection of vendors and live music.

- **West End Farmers Market** - This market is located in the West End neighborhood and is open on Saturdays from May through October. In addition to fresh produce, you can also find artisanal bread, cheese, and other goods.

4

Live Music

Venues

Whether you're in the mood for bluegrass, rock, country, or indie music, there's a live music venue that's perfect for you.

- **Ryman Auditorium** - Known as the "Mother Church of Country Music," the Ryman is an historic gem that has hosted everyone from Johnny Cash to Elvis Presley. With its iconic architecture and rich musical heritage, stepping inside feels like entering a sacred temple for music lovers.

- **Grand Ole Opry** - This iconic venue has been a country music institution since the 1920s and has welcomed some of the biggest names in the genre to its stage. It's a legendary stage that has been graced by the biggest names in the genre, with its iconic circle symbolizing the unbreakable bond between artist and audience. Stepping into the Grand Ole Opry is like stepping into the heart and soul of country music, where tradition meets modern-day magic.

- **Bluebird Cafe** - This intimate venue is a songwriter's paradise, where up-and-coming artists and established performers alike come to share their stories through music.

- **Station Inn** - This bluegrass venue has been a staple in Nashville's music scene for over 40 years and continues to draw crowds with its top-notch musicianship and cozy atmosphere.

- **Mercy Lounge** - This rock club features both local and national acts and is known for its great sound system and lively crowds.

- **Exit/In** - This legendary venue has hosted everyone from The Ramones to The Black Keys and continues to attract a diverse range of artists and fans.

LIVE MUSIC

- **3rd & Lindsley** - This mid-sized venue hosts a variety of genres, from country to rock to blues, and is known for its excellent sound quality and laid-back vibe.

- **The Basement** - This intimate spot is a great place to catch up-and-coming indie artists and singer-songwriters in a cozy setting. With its intimate ambiance and cozy vibes, it's the perfect spot to witness the birth of musical stars, where passionate indie musicians pour their hearts out, creating an enchanting experience that leaves a lasting impression.

- **The Listening Room Cafe** - This one combines great food and drinks with live music from some of Nashville's best songwriters and performers.

- **Dee's Country Cocktail Lounge** - This dive bar in Madison has a retro vibe and a stage that's hosted both up-and-coming and established artists. They serve classic cocktails and Southern-style bar food.

- **Bobby's Idle Hour** - A classic honky-tonk dive bar in the Music Row area, Bobby's is known for its cheap drinks, quirky decor, and live music every night of the week.

- **The 5 Spot** - Located in East Nashville, this unassuming bar hosts a variety of live music, including local and touring acts. On Monday nights, they have a popular dance party called Motown Monday.

- **Exit/In** - has earned legendary status for being one of the most historic rock venues in Nashville. Hosting performances by well-known artists such as The Ramones, Death Cab for Cutie, and Talking Heads, the welcoming crowd and reasonably priced drinks ensure a good time for everyone.

- **The Family Wash** - A neighborhood bar in East Nashville, The Family Wash serves food, drinks, and live music in a cozy atmosphere. They have a stage in the back and a rotating lineup of local artists.

- **Third Man Records Blue Room** - Third Man Records is an independent record label founded by Jack White, known for his band The White Stripes, and has become an integral part of Nashville's music scene. TMR's Blue Room, the only live venue in the world where artists can record their performances direct-to-acetate, hosts an array of performances by artists including Margo Price, Wolf Eyes, Wanda Jackson, and White's own The Dead Weather.

- **The High Watt** - Located in the trendy Cannery Row complex, The High Watt is a small but energetic venue that hosts indie and alternative acts. It's known for its great sound and intimate atmosphere.

- **The End** - A longtime favorite of the local punk and metal scenes, The End is a no-frills venue with a stage, a bar, and a small outdoor patio. They have live music almost every night and the vibe is definitely gritty.

- **The Cobra** - This East Nashville bar has a retro vibe and a lineup of live music that includes rock, punk, and more. They also have karaoke, a patio, and a late-night menu of snacks and pizza.

- **The Sutler Saloon** - A bar and restaurant in the Melrose neighborhood, The Sutler has a stage that's hosted everything from country to soul to rockabilly. They also have a menu of Southern-inspired food and a rooftop bar.

Honky Tonks

"What even *is* a honky tonk?" one might ask.

According to Nashville's Visitor & Convention Bureau, "a honky tonk is an establishment that contains at least one rockin' stage, cold beverages, and live music that lasts all day, every day."

Yes. 7. Days. A. Week.

- **Tootsie's Orchid Lounge** - Known as the "purple building on Broadway," Tootsie's has been a staple of Music City since the 1960s. Legends like Willie Nelson and Patsy Cline have performed here and the bar is famous for its history and charm.

- **Robert's Western World** - This honky tonk is all about traditional country music, with live bands playing classic tunes all day and night. They're also known for their world-famous "Recession Special," which includes a fried bologna sandwich and a PBR.

- **The Stage on Broadway** - The Stage is a three-story honky tonk with a rooftop bar, multiple stages, and live music every day of the week. They're also known for their famous "Sing for Your Supper" program, where customers can sing a song on stage in exchange for a free meal.

LIVE MUSIC

- **Jason Aldean's Kitchen + Rooftop Bar** - Another three-story spot, you'll discover a great view of Broadway from the rooftop bar here, where there tends to be a wait to access after 6 pm. At any hour, the vibe is lively and the service is friendly, with a combination of modern elements and a traditional country feel.

- **Legends Corner** - With a name like Legends Corner, you know this honky tonk is serious about country music. They have live music every day, with bands playing classic country hits from the 60s, 70s, and 80s. They're also known for their extensive collection of country music memorabilia.

- **Honky Tonk Central** - As the name suggests, Honky Tonk Central is a massive honky tonk with three floors, six bars, and live music all day and night. They also have a rooftop bar with great views of downtown Nashville.

- **Nudie's Honky Tonk** - Named after famous western-wear designer Nudie Cohn, this honky tonk is known for its flashy, rhinestone-covered decor. They have live music every day, and you can even grab a bite to eat at their Southern-style restaurant.

- **Layla's Honky Tonk** - Layla's is a cozy, laid-back spot with live music every day and a rooftop patio. They're also known for their delicious hot chicken, which you can order from their full-service kitchen. The bar has a loyal following of regulars and is known for its friendly staff and intimate setting.

- **AJ's Good Time Bar** - Voted the number one honky tonk by *Billboard Magazine*, Alan Jackson's spot where the motto is "keepin' it country", you'll find a cozy atmosphere and plenty of classic country tunes and little rock mixed in. Lots of people come back just for the music.

- **Kid Rock's Big Ass Honky Tonk and Rock n' Roll Steakhouse** - This high-energy place is a wild ride of flavor and entertainment. With sizzling steaks and bands that perform their hearts out and take song requests, it's a non-stop party here.

- **Twelve Thirty Club** - The Justin Timberlake-backed gem is a supper club, honky tonk, and bar known for its sleek design, upscale ambiance, and live entertainment. It offers a luxurious experience for anyone looking to enjoy music, cocktails, and an exclusive-feeling atmosphere with a curated lineup of performances and celebrity allure.

LIVE MUSIC

- **Bootleggers Inn** - It's all about moonshine and live music at this joint. A full bar with a wide selection of moonshine flavors, as well as a stage for live music every day. You can also try their moonshine-infused cocktails and delicious Southern-style food.

- **Legends Corner** - A classic honky tonk on Broadway that draws a mix of tourists and locals with its traditional country music and lively atmosphere. The walls are lined with photos and memorabilia of country music legends, adding to the authentic feel of the place.

- **Famous Nashville** - This one has one of the highest rooftop views in town. Swing by to enjoy the stunning view and catch live performances by some of Nashville's hottest up-and-coming artists.

5

Eat

Breakfast and Brunch

Brunch is not just a meal in Nashville, it's a beloved weekend tradition. In a city that's becoming known for its foodie culture, Nashville brunch spots offer something for everyone, from traditional southern breakfasts to innovative and modern takes on the classics. Combine a lively atmosphere, bottomless mimosas, and live music, and you've got the perfect recipe for a delightful brunch event. With so many options to choose from, brunching in Nashville is not just a meal, it's an experience.

Most of the brunch spots on the list also serve breakfast, but it's best to check the hours of each individual establishment. Some may only serve brunch on weekends or have limited hours during the week. Additionally, most require reservations for breakfast or brunch, so it's always a good idea to call ahead to ensure availability.

- **Adele's** - The brunch paradise you never knew you needed. With a mouthwatering buffet that'll make your taste buds do a happy dance and a trendy but cozy ambiance filled with natural light, it's the perfect place to indulge in some blueberry lemon Johnny cakes and start your day off right.

- **Midtown Cafe** - Rated one of the 50 best southern restaurants in America according to Open Table, here you'll find warm and friendly service at a place that knows how to turn your brunch cravings into a full-blown love affair.

- **Biscuit Love** - This spot is all about southern comfort food with a twist! They offer creative biscuits, brunch cocktails, and locally sourced ingredients. Known to have a line out the door, the vibe is trendy and lively.

- **The Southern** - This downtown hotspot has a chic atmosphere with classic southern dishes and an extensive drink menu. Their shrimp and grits are a must-try.

- **Milk & Honey** - This Instagram-worthy spot offers fresh, modern takes on brunch classics where you can't go wrong with any choice on the menu. With a wide selection of impeccably made coffee and tea drinks to pair with your meal, enjoy a cozy and laid-back vibe with lots of natural light.

- **Kitchen Notes** - Located inside the Omni Hotel, Kitchen Notes has a welcoming, rustic atmosphere and serves up classic southern dishes with a modern twist. The buffet-style brunch is a great way to sample a variety of flavors and dishes.

- **The Row Kitchen & Pub** - The vibe at The Row is cozy and inviting, with classic Southern dishes served up in a comfortable atmosphere. They also have a great selection of craft beer and cocktails.

- **Gray & Dudley** - This trendy spot located inside the 21c Museum Hotel offers an elevated brunch experience with dishes like roasted cauliflower hash and breakfast tacos. The vibe is upscale but relaxed, and the cocktail menu is top-notch.

- **Saint Anejo** - This Mexican-inspired spot offers a brunch menu with a south-of-the-border twist. Enjoy dishes like chilaquiles and breakfast tacos along with a selection of tequila cocktails. The vibe is lively and energetic, so arrive ready to party.

- **The Red Bicycle** - This cozy spot in Germantown offers a friendly atmosphere and delicious breakfast and brunch dishes, such as huevos rancheros and waffles with a great selection of coffee drinks.

- **Loveless Cafe** - This Nashville institution has been serving up southern-style breakfast and brunch since 1951. Their famous biscuits and homemade preserves are a must-try! The vibe is rustic and downhome country, with plenty of southern hospitality.

- **The Old School** - This quaint spot in Germantown offers classic brunch dishes such as pancakes and eggs benedict, along with a selection of craft cocktails. The vibe is cozy and intimate, perfect for a laid-back weekend brunch.

- **Proper Bagel** - This East Nashville spot makes some of the best bagels in town, and their brunch menu includes mouth-watering sandwiches like the Hangover Bagel and the Lox Bagel. The vibe is casual and cozy.

- **The Sutler** - This Southern-inspired restaurant and bar in Melrose has a brunch menu filled with classics like biscuits and gravy, shrimp and grits, and chicken and waffles. The vibe is lively and welcoming, with live music on weekends.

- **Liberty Common** - Located in downtown Nashville, this French brasserie offers a brunch menu that combines classic French dishes with Southern flavors. Don't miss the Croque Madame or the avocado toast. The vibe is chic and sophisticated.

- **Hemingway's Bar & Hideaway** - This cozy bar in Wedgewood-Houston offers a brunch menu that's as delicious as it is unique. Try the Eggs in Purgatory or the Chilaquiles Verdes, and wash it down with a creative cocktail or craft beer. The vibe is laid-back and welcoming, with a rustic, industrial feel.

- **The Grilled Cheeserie Melt Shop** - This food truck turned brick-and-mortar restaurant in Hillsboro Village specializes in grilled cheese sandwiches, but their brunch menu is just as impressive. Try the Monte Cristo or the Cheesy Hash Brown Melt, and don't forget a side of tater tots. The vibe is fun and quirky, with a retro feel.

- **Josephine** - This cozy neighborhood spot in 12South offers a brunch menu that's both creative and comforting. Highlights include the Fried Chicken Biscuit, the Shakshuka, and the Breakfast Flatbread. The vibe is intimate and relaxed, with warm lighting and a rustic feel.

- **Urban Cowboy Public House** - This chic restaurant and bar in East Nashville offers a brunch menu that's both elevated and approachable. Don't miss the Blueberry Ricotta Pancakes or the Avocado Toast with Crab. The vibe is stylish and sophisticated, with a touch of Southern charm.

- **Nadeen's Hermitage Haven** - This family-owned spot in Hermitage offers a brunch menu filled with Southern classics like biscuits and gravy, chicken and waffles, and shrimp and grits. The vibe is cozy and welcoming, with friendly service and home-cooked flavors.

Dinner

Get ready to embark on a foodie adventure, because this city knows how to bring the flavor! Whether you're in the mood for Southern comfort food, international flavors, or gourmet creations, Nashville's diverse dining scene promises an unforgettable culinary journey that showcases the city's passion for food and hospitality.

There are far too many unique and delectable restaurants to name, so here are some highlights in no particular order:

- **Husk** - Known for its elevated southern cuisine, Husk sources all of its ingredients from within a 100-mile radius of the restaurant. The menu changes daily and features dishes like braised pork shoulder and skillet cornbread.

- **The Catbird Seat** - This intimate, 22-seat restaurant offers a unique dining experience with an open kitchen and an ever-changing tasting menu. The chefs interact with diners throughout the meal, creating a personalized experience.

- **Black Tap** - This is the place to indulge in juicy burgers, over-the-top shakes, and even boozy shake shots, conveniently located near downtown's honky tonks and music venues. While the menu features favorites from their other locations, expect exclusive locally-inspired items like the Tennessee Burger with Jack Daniel's red pepper jam, pickles, sweet potato chips, white BBQ sauce, and chopped parsley.

- **Present Tense** - Located in the Wedgewood-Houston neighborhood is a Japanese-inspired eatery operated by Michelin-starred veterans, offering an intimate omakase experience and a sake bar. Their menu features shareable small plates influenced by Japan and Southeast Asia, including aged tuna tartare on grilled seaweed sourdough and inventive brunch options like Japanese soufflé pancakes and a twist on chicken and waffles.

- **Rolf and Daughters** - Located in Germantown, Rolf and Daughters offers a creative, Mediterranean-inspired menu featuring dishes like ricotta gnocchi and lamb ragu. The atmosphere is relaxed yet refined.

- **City House** - This Germantown staple is known for its Italian-inspired dishes with a southern twist. The pizza, made in a wood-fired oven, is a must-try, as are the pastas and house-cured meats.

- **The Chef and I** - This unique restaurant offers a chef's table experience with a rotating cast of chefs and a 12-course tasting menu. You can watch the chefs prepare the dishes while they enjoy your meal.

- **Heirloom** - The new rooftop bar at Holston House in Nashville, combines a penthouse garden vibe with Southern tapas, offering panoramic views, open-air lounge seating, fire pits, and delicious bites. Their menu highlights vibrant produce from local purveyors, featuring dishes like fried green tomatoes, charred onion hummus, cast iron steak, and a delightful "Farmer's Platter" with seasonal veggie delights.

- **Lockeland Table** - This East Nashville restaurant offers southern-inspired dishes made with locally sourced ingredients. The menu changes seasonally and features dishes like bacon-wrapped pork tenderloin and blackened catfish.

- **White Limozeen** - Step into a Dolly Parton dreamland! Located on the rooftop of the Graduate hotel, its pink paradise vibes, palm trees, and dazzling decor gives all the glam. Sip on delicious cocktails, savor Southern-inspired dishes, and soak in the panoramic views of the city while feeling like a true country superstar. It's the perfect spot to bring your friends, take photos and live your best Dolly-inspired life.

- **Etch** - Located downtown, Etch offers a modern take on American cuisine. The menu features dishes like octopus with harissa and grilled lamb chops with mint chimichurri. The restaurant also has an extensive wine list.

- **Josephine** - This 12South neighborhood restaurant offers a menu of contemporary American cuisine. Dishes like beef tenderloin with smoked potatoes and trout with quinoa make for a memorable meal.

- **The Farm House** - This farm-to-table restaurant in downtown

Nashville features locally sourced ingredients and an ever-changing menu. The dishes are classic with a southern twist, like shrimp and grits and fried chicken.

- **House of Cards** - Uncover an extraordinary underground venue offering a truly unique dining and entertainment experience. Journey through secret tunnels to a mesmerizing world adorned with a hand-crafted bar, a multimillion-dollar art collection, European antiques, and captivating magic-related artifacts and performances.

- **Butcher & Bee** - Known for its Mediterranean-inspired dishes made with locally sourced ingredients, Butcher & Bee offers a creative menu that changes daily. The atmosphere is casual and welcoming.

- **Urban Grub** - This contemporary Southern restaurant in 12South offers a lively atmosphere and a diverse menu that includes everything from fresh seafood to wood-fired pizzas. Don't miss their famous oysters, which are shucked to order at the raw bar.

- **Sinema** - Housed in a beautifully restored movie theater in the Melrose neighborhood, Sinema serves up elevated Southern cuisine in a stunning, glamorous setting. The menu changes often, but you can always expect creative, beautifully plated dishes that are almost too pretty to eat.

- **Chauhan Ale & Masala House** - Celebrity chef Maneet Chauhan's restaurant offers a unique blend of Indian and Southern cuisine in a chic, modern setting. Don't miss the chicken tikka poutine or the butter chicken meatballs.

- **Josephine** - This sleek, modern restaurant in 12South focuses on contemporary American cuisine with a seasonal, farm-to-table approach. Standout dishes include the truffle mac and cheese and the wood-fired octopus.

- **Etch** - Chef Deb Paquette's downtown restaurant offers a sophisticated, globally inspired menu that draws from a variety of cuisines. Dishes like the roasted beet salad with whipped feta and the duck confit with sweet potato hash are not to be missed.

- **The Southern** - Located in the heart of downtown Nashville, The Southern serves up elevated Southern cuisine in a stylish, modern setting. Don't miss the hot chicken sliders, the shrimp and grits, or the fried green tomatoes.

- **Virago** - With its sleek, exclusive feel and modern Japanese cuisine, Virago is a go-to destination for sushi enthusiasts and those seeking a sophisticated dining experience that combines traditional flavors with contemporary twists.

- **Saint Anejo** - This vibrant Mexican eatery impresses with its lively atmosphere, extensive tequila selection, and mouthwatering menu of tacos, enchiladas, and flavorful margaritas, making it a must-visit for Mexican food lovers.

- **The Rosewall**: An upscale lounge and dining space offering a sophisticated ambiance with a menu that features a fusion of American and European flavors, showcasing seasonal ingredients and culinary expertise in an elegant setting.

- **Kayne Prime**: This premier steakhouse provides a luxurious dining experience, serving top-quality cuts of beef in an upscale and refined setting. From perfectly aged steaks to delectable seafood options and indulgent sides, Kayne Prime is a top choice for discerning steak enthusiasts.

6

Drink

Bars (The Ones that Aren't Honky Tonks)

When most people think of Nashville, Broadway comes to mind. However, "NashVegas" (and the bachelor/bachelorette capital of the US) is simply its alter-ego, where the rowdy honky tonks and pedal taverns reign supreme. As fun a scene as it can be, reducing Nashville to this small sliver really does the city a grave disservice! There are many incredible bars that offer a diverse and vibrant scene beyond the famous Broadway strip and traditional dives. From trendy cocktail lounges to upscale wine bars, you'll find a wide range of options to suit any mood.

- **The Patterson House** - Step into this speakeasy-style cocktail bar where phones are heavily discouraged, and be transported to the Prohibition era. With skilled mixologists crafting unique and delicious drinks, The Patterson House offers a sophisticated and intimate atmosphere for cocktail enthusiasts.

- **Bastion** - Located in a converted storage space, Bastion is a hip and trendy spot known for its innovative cocktails and exceptional food. The bar features a rotating menu of creative libations and a cozy, laid-back ambiance.

- **Skull's Rainbow Room** - Step inside this hidden gem and immerse yourself in a cozy, retro vibe with a lively atmosphere that takes you back to the golden era of nightlife. A Nashville staple since 1948, here you'll find a modern, classy speakeasy where you can enjoy delicious cocktails, tasty bites, and live entertainment.

- **Red Phone Booth** - A speakeasy worth the hype, step inside an actual phone booth to access the place, *if* you know the code. From the mystique of gaining entry to extensive cocktail and cigar list, this hidden gem will not disappoint.

- **The Fox Bar & Cocktail Club** - Tucked away in East Nashville, The Fox Bar & Cocktail Club exudes old-world charm and offers a menu of expertly crafted cocktails. The cozy, vintage-inspired space invites you to relax and enjoy a drink from their extensive selection.

- **Pearl Diver** - A tropical oasis in the heart of Nashville, Pearl Diver specializes in tiki-inspired cocktails and an island-themed atmosphere. The bar boasts an extensive rum collection and serves up refreshing and exotic drinks that transport you to a beachside paradise.

- **Pinewood Social** - You simply cannot go wrong here for breakfast, brunch, lunch or dinner. With a relaxing, trendy atmosphere that doesn't take itself too seriously, they even have bowling lanes available to reserve as well as a bocce ball court outside with plenty of seating. Don't forget to have your parking validated if you park on the adjacent deck.

- **No. 308** - This East Nashville neighborhood bar is known for its welcoming vibe and expertly crafted cocktails. With a menu that spans from classic to creative concoctions, No. 308 offers a diverse selection of drinks to suit every palate.

- **Layer Cake** - This colorful, high-energy four-story spot is right around the corner from Bridgestone, and a great place to stop for killer handmade cocktails and, you guessed it, a piece of cake. Excellent food and service to match.

- **Black Rabbit** - A large restaurant and one of the more intimate bar settings in Downtown Nashville, they focus on small plates intended to be shared among friends. Great place to stop in for Happy Hour, Monday through Saturday, with $5 cocktails, $2 off draft beer, and 2-for-1 domestics.

- **Urban Cowboy Public House** - Combining a bar and a cozy neighborhood gathering place, Urban Cowboy Public House offers craft cocktails, a curated whiskey list, and a laid-back atmosphere. The rustic and stylish decor adds to the charm of this East Nashville gem.

- **Attaboy** - A hidden gem in East Nashville, Attaboy is a speakeasy-style bar that prides itself on personalized and inventive cocktails. Guests can chat with the skilled bartenders, share their preferences, and let the mixologists work their magic.

- **The Green Hour** - Inspired by the Parisian tradition of "l'heure verte," The Green Hour is an absinthe-focused bar that takes you on a journey through the intriguing world of the green spirit. The bar offers a unique and immersive experience for absinthe lovers and cocktail enthusiasts alike.

- **Old Glory** - Housed in a former boiler room, Old Glory is a quirky and upscale cocktail lounge that showcases an impressive selection of spirits. With a focus on classic cocktails and a sophisticated ambiance, Old Glory provides an elegant setting for an evening of drinks and conversation.

Dives

Calling all outside-the-box visitors: make sure to explore Nashville's dive bars for a fun and laid-back experience that captures the city's authentic spirit. These hidden gems serve up a lively and unpretentious atmosphere where you can mingle with locals, discover local music talents, and indulge in deliciously cheap drinks. From the quirky decor to the friendly bartenders, Nashville's dive bars are a must-visit for anyone seeking a unique and offbeat nightlife experience.

- **Dino's** - A classic Nashville spot, complete with a jukebox, cheap beer, and a cozy atmosphere.

- **Santa's Pub** - Located in a trailer, this Christmas-themed dive is known for its 7-days-a-week karaoke and funky decor, which includes a sleigh and a giant Santa statue.

- **The Crying Wolf** - A wide selection of beer and whiskey can be found here, as well as live music and a patio with fire pits for chilly nights.

- **Duke's** - This East Nashville dive has a reputation for strong drinks, a welcoming atmosphere, and some of the best bar food in the city.

- **Springwater Supper Club & Lounge** - This classic has been around since 1896 and offers cheap drinks, live music, and a laid-back atmosphere that feels like home.

- **The Villager Tavern** - A neighborhood spot that's been around since the 1950s, offering a friendly atmosphere, cold drinks, and a jukebox that's always cranking out classic tunes.

- **Fran's East Side** - A favorite among locals for its strong drinks, cozy atmosphere, and occasional karaoke nights.

- **Bobby's Idle Hour Tavern** - Bobby's is a classic Music Row dive bar that's been around since 1958, offering a laid-back atmosphere, live music, and cheap beer.

- **Mickey's Tavern** - Mickey's Tavern is a no-frills dive bar that knows what it is and doesn't pretend to be anything else. You won't find any karaoke or live music here, but you will find cheap drinks, pool tables, darts, and a killer jukebox. Plus, it's one of the few dive bars in Nashville that's smoke-free.

- **Twin Kegs** - Not to be confused with Twin Kegs II, the slightly less divey version of the two, the dim lighting and haze of smoke create the perfect atmosphere for shuffleboard and cheap beer with a cast of friendly regulars known as "Keggers." Some folks say Twin Kegs has the best burger in town, but I'll steer clear of controversy and let Burger Up and other top contenders hash it out.

- **American Legion Post 82** - This ain't just any American Legion. It's a historic spot where vets used to gather for cold brews and casual chats. It's also where Nashvillians of all ages come to shake a leg at Honky Tonk Tuesdays, featuring free shows and rotating musical acts. According to the local singer Tanya Montana Coe, "Honky Tonk Tuesdays is a good ol' time that takes us back to the Nashville we know and love. No need to get fancy here. It's like a cozy blanket for us country folks."

Breweries

Beer enthusiasts rejoice. Don't miss the chance to explore the thriving brewery scene in Nashville, where you'll find an abundance of craft breweries. From hoppy IPAs to rich stouts and refreshing sours, these breweries offer a wide range of flavors and styles that cater to every beer lover's palate. Immerse yourself in the vibrant atmosphere, engage with passionate brewers, and sip on locally crafted brews that showcase the city's creativity and dedication to the art of brewing. Cheers to discovering new flavors and experiencing the true essence of Nashville's beer culture!

- **Bearded Iris Brewing** - Known for its IPAs and hazy beers, Bearded Iris is the perfect spot for hop heads. Plus, their taproom is pet-friendly, so you can enjoy a cold one with your furry best friend.

- **Southern Grist Brewing** - With creative and experimental brews, Southern Grist always keeps it interesting. Their taprooms feature rotating food trucks, so you can pair your beer with some delicious bites.

- **Tennessee Brew Works** - From their classic Southern Wit to their limited edition sours, Tennessee Brew Works has something for every taste. Stop by their taproom for live music and tasty bites from their on-site restaurant.

- **Black Abbey Brewing** - This Belgian-inspired brewery is known for its rich, full-bodied beers. Their taproom has a cozy, monastery-like feel and features live music and events throughout the week.

- **Jackalope Brewing Company** - Home of the popular Thunder Ann IPA, Jackalope also offers seasonal and limited edition beers. Their taproom is a great spot for hanging with friends and playing some board games.

- **TailGate Beer** - With a massive outdoor space, TailGate is the perfect spot for enjoying a beer and some yard games. They offer a wide range of brews, from classic lagers to funky sours.

- **East Nashville Beer Works** - This neighborhood brewery is all about community, with regular events and partnerships with local organizations. Their beers range from light and refreshing to bold and hoppy.

- **Little Harpeth Brewing** - With a focus on traditional German brewing techniques, here you'll find a unique selection of lagers and pilsners. Their taproom has a laid-back vibe and features a rotating selection of food trucks. Try their flagship Chicken Scratch Pilsner or their seasonal Oktoberfest brew while hanging out in their inviting taproom.

- **Smith & Lentz Brewing** - This family-owned brewery is known for their German-inspired beers and creative small-batch brews. Their taproom has a cozy, intimate feel and features regular events like trivia and game nights.

- **Mantra Artisan Ales** - This small batch brewery in Franklin is dedicated to brewing unique and flavorful beers with a focus on Belgian-style ales. Swing by their taproom for a pint of their popular Saffron IPA or a seasonal brew.

- **New Heights Brewing Company** - Another family-owned brewery in East Nashville that offers a variety of craft beers with creative flavors like Lemon Basil Saison and Blueberry Wheat. They also have a great patio area for enjoying a cold one on a sunny day.

- **Mill Creek Brewing Co.** - Mill Creek is a popular brewery in Nolensville known for their award-winning beers like the Lil Darlin' blonde ale and the Woodshed IPA. They also offer a tasty food menu and a spacious taproom perfect for groups.

- **Fat Bottom Brewing Co.** - Fat Bottom is a well-known brewery in East Nashville that offers a range of craft beers with fun names like Ruby, Ida, and Black Betty. They also have a great outdoor space for enjoying a pint with friends and family.

- **Mayday Brewery** - This Murfreesboro brewery is a fun and quirky spot to enjoy a cold beer and some live music. Try their flagship Angry Redhead IPA or one of their rotating seasonal brews while hanging out in their colorful taproom.

- **Honky Tonk Brewing Co.** - A fun-loving brewery that doesn't take itself too seriously, this one is located in downtown Nashville and known for its sours and IPAs. Swing by for a pint of their own Cherry Berliner Weisse while enjoying some live music or a game of cornhole.

Vineyards

If you're down for a true Nashville adventure, and also searching for the top wineries in the area, these vineyards are the ultimate kickoff point. Indulge in the local wine scene and discover a variety of flavorful wines crafted with passion and expertise. From sipping on smooth reds to savoring crisp whites, these vineyards offer a unique opportunity to taste Tennessee's finest wines while enjoying the picturesque beauty of the vineyards themselves. Whether you're a connoisseur or simply looking to unwind with a glass of wine, exploring the vineyards in the Nashville area is an exquisite experience that promises to leave you with an appreciation for the region's winemaking traditions.

- **Arrington Vineyards** - Owned by country music star Kix Brooks, Arrington Vineyards has a wide selection of award-winning wines and a beautiful vineyard setting perfect for a picnic and some good vibes. Bring the kids and enjoy plenty of room to stretch out and relax.

- **Beachaven Vineyards and Winery** - This winery has a relaxed and fun atmosphere, with live music on weekends and a large outdoor patio. Their award-winning wines are made with locally sourced fruit and their tasting room is a great place to unwind.

- **Belle Meade Winery** - Housed in a historic 19th-century mansion,

Belle Meade Winery has a wide selection of wines made from grapes grown in their own vineyard. Take a tour of the mansion and the winery, or just relax on their spacious lawn with a glass of wine.

- **City Winery Nashville** - This urban winery and music venue is located in the heart of downtown Nashville. Enjoy a glass of wine while watching a live performance in their intimate concert space.

- **Grinder's Switch Winery** - Located in the rolling hills of Middle Tennessee, Grinder's offers a wide selection of wines made with locally grown grapes. Take a tour of their beautiful vineyards and enjoy a tasting in their cozy tasting room.

- **Long Hollow Winery** - This family-owned winery is located in the scenic countryside just outside of Nashville. Their award-winning wines are made with grapes grown on their own estate, and their laid-back tasting room is the perfect place to relax and unwind.

- **Natchez Hills Vineyard** - Nestled in the picturesque hills of Tennessee, Natchez Hills offers a wide selection of handcrafted wines and stunning views of the surrounding countryside. Their tasting room is a great place to sample their wines and enjoy a relaxing afternoon.

- **Sumner Crest Winery** - This charming winery is located in the heart of downtown Portland, Tennessee. Their wines are made with grapes grown on their own estate, and their tasting room is a great place to enjoy a glass of wine and some good company.

- **Tenn South Distillery and Winery** - This unique winery and distillery offers a wide selection of award-winning wines and spirits. Take a tour of their facility and sample some of their delicious products in their tasting room.

- **White Squirrel Winery** - This family-owned winery is located just outside of Nashville and offers a wide selection of wines made with locally sourced fruit. Their tasting room is a great place to relax and enjoy a glass of wine while taking in the beautiful scenery.

Distilleries

Tennessee is the birthplace of whiskey, and some of the best distilleries are located right here in Nashville. There are several a bit further out, but you can't put a list of distilleries together and not include the ones below. From classic Tennessee whiskey to flavored moonshines, there's a distillery for everyone. Here are some of the best distilleries to check out, in order of distance from Nashville, with the exception of the first and, undoubtedly, most significant one:

- **Nearest Green Distillery** - This place's namesake holds great significance in the world of whiskey as the best whiskey maker that the world *never* knew for many years. Nathan "Nearest" Green, a formerly enslaved African American master distiller, mentored and taught a young Jack Daniel, who would go on to become a legendary whiskey maker. The Uncle Nearest Distillery, established in 2017 and headquartered in Shelbyville, honors the legacy of Nearest Green by producing premium Tennessee whiskey and showcasing his influential role in whiskey-making history. The distillery not only celebrates Green's craftsmanship but also serves as a platform for promoting diversity, inclusion, and recognition of African American contributions to the spirits industry. Uncle Nearest whiskey is now celebrated worldwide, and the distillery – which also happens to house the world's longest (518-foot) bar, stands as a testament to the rich heritage he created.

- **Corsair Distillery** - A stone's throw from downtown Nashville (just 2 miles), here you'll find a one-of-a-kind selection of whiskey and spirits that are sure to tantalize your taste buds. Be sure to try their award-winning Triple Smoke and Ryemageddon whiskeys.

- **Nelson's Green Brier Distillery** - Just 6 miles from the heart of Nashville lies an historic distillery that was resurrected by brothers Andy and Charlie Nelson. You absolutely cannot leave without tasting their signature Belle Meade Bourbon.

- **Pennington Distilling Co.** - Around 14 miles southeast of downtown Nashville in Antioch is where a variety of spirits is crafted, including their Davidson Reserve Bourbon, which has won numerous awards. It's a must-try for any whiskey aficionado.

- **H. Clark Distillery** - Nestled in Thompson's Station, about 30 miles south of Nashville, they create handcrafted spirits in small batches. Be sure to try their Tennessee Dry Gin and Black & Tan Whiskey.

- **Short Mountain Distillery** - Situated in Woodbury, an hour's drive from Nashville, Short Mountain produces small-batch, organic moonshine, bourbon, and Tennessee whiskey using all the traditional techniques. Take a tour of the distillery and be sure to take in the stunning surrounding area while you're there.

- **Leiper's Fork Distillery** - About 40 miles southwest of Nashville, in the little country town of Leiper's Fork, this distillery offers tours and tastings of their handcrafted spirits. Definitely sample both their award-winning Tennessee Whiskey and Bourbon.

- **George Dickel Distillery** - Just 70 miles southeast of Nashville, in Tullahoma, this historic place has been crafting high-quality

Tennessee whiskey since 1870 and is a must-visit for whiskey enthusiasts. Join one of their tours to see firsthand how they make their world-renowned whiskey.

- **Jack Daniel's Distillery** - In Lynchburg, just 70 miles southeast of Nashville, lies perhaps the most famous of them all: the legendary Jack Daniel's Distillery. Take a tour of the distillery and discover the secrets behind this famous Tennessee whiskey. It's a true American icon that you cannot miss.

- **Prichard's Distillery** - Located about 100 miles southwest of Nashville in Kelso, Prichard's produces top-quality rums and whiskeys. Don't forget to sample their range of spirits, and take a tour of their distillery to see how they make their world-class beverages.

- **Chattanooga Whiskey Co.** - About 130 miles southeast of Nashville, in picturesque Chattanooga, lies the Chattanooga Whiskey Co. This spot produces a range of whiskeys, including their signature Tennessee High Malt. Take a tour of the distillery and enjoy tastings of their spirits, it's a perfect day trip!

7

Sports

Football

The Tennessee Titans are a pro football powerhouse. This team calls Nashville home and they've been crushing it since they hit the scene in '97. If you haven't been to one of their games, you're missing out on some serious fun.

Nissan Stadium is their home turf, which sits pretty in downtown Nashville right by the Cumberland River. This open-air stadium is huge and can hold up to 69,143 screaming fans. With views of the skyline, the game is as exciting to watch as it is to feel. And trust me, you'll feel it. The electric energy from the blue and white-wearing fans, the music, and the pre-game tailgating will have you feeling all the love for the Titans.

But before you start thinking about the food and drinks, you should know parking can be a bit of a hassle, so it's best to arrive early and reserve your spot. And, of course, you can't forget about the tailgating! Bring your friends, your cooler, and your appetite. Inside the stadium, get ready to feast on some seriously tasty local eats, like hot chicken and BBQ.

It's important to note that security measures are in place, so be sure to brush up on the stadium's guidelines before you go. But once you're inside, you'll be instantly swept up in the excitement of the game. Cheering on the Titans, participating in the chants, and definitely joining in on the wave is all part of the experience.

Titans games are an absolute blast that will have you feeling like a true Nashvillian. So grab your game-day gear, get pumped up, and prepare to join the sea of passionate fans as you cheer on the Titans with all your might. Don't miss out on this electrifying event that encapsulates the city's sports culture and brings people together for an unforgettable game-day spectacle.

Hockey

Saddle up, because Bridgestone Arena is rumored to be the loudest arena in the NHL, and we brag about it...a lot. There isn't a bad seat in the house at this venue located right in the heart of downtown Nashville, and it holds up to 17,500 very enthusiastic fans. This team is the pride and joy of Music City, and attending a game is an experience you don't want to miss.

The arena has a raucous, high-energy atmosphere that's contagious. From the loud music to the impressive pre-game show, the excitement is palpable before the puck even drops. Once the game begins, fans cheer on their team, participate in chants, and even toss the occasional catfish onto the ice!

If you're planning to attend a Predators game (or "Preds" as we locals call them), be sure to arrive early to soak up the fun. Parking can be a bit of a challenge, so consider using public transportation or ride-share services. You'll want to come hungry, as the arena offers a wide variety of delicious food and drink options.

Once you're inside Bridgestone Arena, be prepared to have a blast. You'll find plenty of interactive exhibits, games, and activities to keep you entertained during intermission. And of course, the game itself is a thrilling display of athleticism and skill. Whether you're a die-hard hockey fan or a newcomer to the sport, you're sure to have a blast cheering on the Nashville Predators.

Baseball

The Nashville Sounds are Nashville's minor league baseball team. Going to a Sounds game is, of course, an all-American pastime that's fun for the whole family (*1940s radio voice). The team plays at First Horizon Park, a state-of-the-art stadium located in downtown Nashville that seats up to 10,000 fans.

The Sounds are part of the Triple-A Pacific Coast League and have been a Nashville staple since 1978. Attending a game is a great way to experience the excitement of baseball and soak up the local culture. Fans can expect to enjoy classic ballpark food like hot dogs, popcorn, and peanuts, as well as local craft beer and cocktails.

First Horizon Park is located in the heart of the Germantown neighborhood, an area that's home to some of the city's best restaurants and bars. Fans can grab a bite to eat before or after the game, and enjoy the vibrant energy of this bustling neighborhood.

The grass berm seating area is a great spot for families to enjoy the game with plenty of room to run around and stretch out. Unlike traditional stadium seats, the grass berm provides a more relaxed environment where kids can lay on blankets or sit down and even stand up or assume whichever posture kids prefer. While some teams may have stricter rules, it's not uncommon to see kids running around and having fun on the berm, especially when it's not too crowded.

To make the most out of your Sounds game experience, be sure to arrive early and take advantage of the pre-game festivities. There's often live music, games, and other entertainment before the first pitch. And if you're a die-hard fan, be sure to check out the team store for some sweet Sounds merch.

Overall, attending a Nashville Sounds game is a must-do for anyone visiting. It's a great change of pace, and an affordable way to experience the excitement of baseball, while also getting a taste of the city's unique culture and local flavor.

Soccer

The Nashville Soccer Club is Nashville's own professional soccer team. This newer addition to Nashville's sports scene has quickly gained a loyal following among locals and visitors alike. Attending a game is an experience like no other, with plenty of action on the field and a lively atmosphere in the stands.

The team shares Nissan Stadium with the Titans, located in the heart of downtown Nashville along the beautiful Cumberland River. With a seating capacity of over 69,000, there's plenty of room for fans to come and cheer on their team. The stadium is easily accessible by car or public transportation, and there are plenty of parking options available.

Once you're inside the stadium, get ready for a fun and high-energy experience. The Nashville Soccer Club has a passionate fan base, known as The Assembly, who bring plenty of energy and enthusiasm to every game. The team's colors are gold and navy, and you'll see plenty of fans decked out in team gear and waving flags throughout the game.

When it comes to planning your visit, there are a few things to keep in mind. Arrive early to soak up the pregame atmosphere and grab some food and drinks from the stadium vendors. The Nashville Soccer Club also offers a variety of ticket options, from single-game tickets to season tickets, so you can choose the option that works best for you. And don't forget to bring your team spirit and join in on the chants and cheers with The Assembly.

Attending a Nashville Soccer Club game is a thrilling way to dive into Nashville's sports scene and connect with the local community.

It's an electrifying experience that allows you to fully embrace the passion and talent of the players while immersing yourself in the vibrant atmosphere. So, gear up, join the enthusiastic crowd, and get ready for an unforgettable soccer showdown that will leave you captivated and fuel your love for the game.

8

Hike

Whether you're a seasoned hiker or just looking for an easy day trip with the kids, Tennessee's trails and waterfalls are sure to leave you in awe and feeling inspired. These places provide the perfect setting for hiking, camping, fishing, or simply immersing yourself in the wonders of nature with their diverse landscapes and abundant wildlife. I invite you to grab your hiking boots, pack a picnic, and get ready to experience the stunning beauty of the lush forests, rolling hills, and breathtaking waterfalls.

State Parks and Waterfalls

In order of distance from Nashville:

- **Radnor Lake State Park** - Located around 8 miles south of Nashville, Radnor Lake is a nature lover's paradise. It offers over 1,300 acres of protected wilderness and is home to a variety of wildlife, including bald eagles.

- **Long Hunter State Park** - Located around 20 miles east of Nashville, this park offers boating, fishing, and hiking opportunities. It features over 26 miles of trails and access to Percy Priest Lake.

- **Cedars of Lebanon State Park** - Located 35 miles east of Nashville, this park is named for its unique cedar glades. It offers over eight miles of hiking trails and ample camping and picnic areas.

- **Montgomery Bell State Park** - Located 40 miles west of Nashville, this park is popular for camping, hiking, and fishing. Visitors can explore over 20 miles of hiking trails and enjoy the 135-acre lake.

- **Henry Horton State Park** - Located 50 miles south of Nashville, this park boasts a beautiful golf course and scenic trails. Visitors can hike on over 10 miles of trails and enjoy the park's 18-hole golf course.

- **Burgess Falls State Park** - About 75 miles east, this 1.5-mile hike features not one, but four waterfalls. The moderate difficulty level takes you through scenic trails and offers breathtaking views as the path keeps you right next to the water for the duration of the hike.

- **Machine Falls** - Located approximately 75 southeast, this 1.6-mile hike leads to a stunning 60-foot waterfall. With a moderate difficulty level hike, it offers a peaceful escape and great photo opportunities.

- **Old Stone Fort State Archaeological Park** - Located 75 miles southeast, the Old Stone Fort was built over 1,500 years ago, and served as a ceremonial gathering place for Native Americans. Today, Old Stone Fort offers scenic hiking trails that showcase the fort's walls, stunning waterfalls, and informative panels about its history.

- **Cummins Falls State Park** - Around 80 miles east, this 2.5-mile hike leads to a stunning waterfall. With a moderate difficulty level, it's great for families and offers swimming opportunities at the base of the falls.

- **Rock Island State Park** - Located 85 miles east of Nashville, this park showcases cascading waterfalls and scenic overlooks. Visitors can hike on over 10 miles of trails and enjoy fishing and swimming.

- **South Cumberland State Park** - Around 90 miles southeast of Nashville, this park is a haven for outdoor enthusiasts. It offers over 90 miles of trails, including the famous Fiery Gizzard Trail, camping options, and fishing opportunities.

- **Twin Falls at Rock Island State Park** - Located approximately 90 miles east, this 1-mile hike unveils two beautiful waterfalls. Along this moderate difficulty level trail, you can soak in the beauty of the Caney Fork River, and take a refreshing swim.

- **Lost Creek Falls** - About 100 miles east, this 1.5-mile hike rewards you with a beautiful 40-foot waterfall. This moderate difficulty level trail showcases scenic hills and valleys.

- **Foster Falls** - Also around 100 southeast, this 1.5-mile hike takes you to a magnificent 60-foot waterfall. With a moderate difficulty level, it offers beautiful views of the cascading water and is a popular spot for rock climbing.

- **Virgin Falls** - Approximately 120 miles east, this 9-mile hike takes you to a stunning 110-foot waterfall. This trail is considered difficult and is recommended for slightly more experienced hikers, providing a challenging adventure in a remote setting.

- **Fall Creek Falls State Park** - Located slightly further east, 125 miles east, this hike boasts the tallest waterfall in the Eastern United States at 256 feet. With over 26,000 acres of wilderness, it offers various trails and scenic overlooks.

- **Piney Falls State Natural Area** - Located approximately 130 miles east, this 1-mile hike leads to a beautiful 80-foot waterfall. With a moderate difficulty level, it offers beautiful forest views and wildlife sightings.

- **Ruby Falls** - This unique 145-foot underground waterfall is located in Chattanooga, 130 miles southeast. It is a popular tourist destination and offers guided tours of the cave system that leads to the waterfall.

State and National Forests

Tennessee's state and national forests are a haven for nature enthusiasts and outdoor adventurers alike. With vast stretches of pristine wilderness, these forests offer endless opportunities for hiking, camping, fishing, and wildlife watching. Whether you're seeking solitude or adventure, Tennessee's forests are a natural playground waiting to be discovered.

- **Chickasaw State Forest** - Located in western Tennessee, this forest covers over 15,000 acres and features hiking trails, fishing opportunities, and a variety of wildlife. It's about a 1.5-hour drive from Nashville.

- **Natchez Trace State Forest** - Located in the western part of the state, this forest covers over 48,000 acres and features hiking, fishing, and hunting opportunities. It's about a 2-hour drive from Nashville.

- **Land Between the Lakes National Recreation Area** - Located on the border between Tennessee and Kentucky, this 170,000-acre forest features numerous opportunities for outdoor recreation, including hiking, fishing, and wildlife viewing. It's about a 2-hour drive from Nashville.

- **Big South Fork National River and Recreation Area** - Located in northeastern Tennessee, this forest covers over 125,000 acres and features scenic river gorges, sandstone bluffs, and numerous hiking and horseback riding trails. It's about a 3-hour drive from Nashville.

- **Daniel Boone National Forest** - Located in southeastern Kentucky and eastern Tennessee, this 700,000-acre forest offers opportunities for hiking, camping, and fishing. It's about a 3-hour drive from Nashville.

- **Cherokee National Forest** - Located in eastern Tennessee, this forest covers over 650,000 acres and features numerous hiking trails, waterfalls, and campsites. It's about a 3.5-hour drive from Nashville.

Lakes

Middle Tennessee is home to some of the most beautiful and serene lakes in the country. Whether you're looking to fish, swim, boat, or just relax on the shore, the lakes in this region have got you covered.

- **Percy Priest Lake** - Located just 10 miles east of Nashville, Percy Priest Lake is a popular destination for fishing, boating, and swimming. With over 14,000 acres of water, this lake is perfect for water sports and recreation. The lake is surrounded by parks and campgrounds, making it a great place to spend a weekend.

- **Old Hickory Lake** - Spanning over 22,000 acres and boasting 97 miles of shoreline, Old Hickory is a beautiful reservoir that provides a peaceful escape from city life. Located 15 miles northeast of Nashville, this lake is a popular spot for fishing, kayaking, and bird watching. Visitors can explore the lake's many islands and coves, or relax on one of the many beaches.

- **Center Hill Lake** - Located about 70 miles east of Nashville, Center Hill Lake is a pristine mountain lake with crystal-clear waters and multiple coves and inlets. The lake spans over 18,000 acres and is surrounded by rugged cliffs and rolling hills. Visitors can enjoy swimming, boating, and fishing, or explore the many hiking trails in the area.

- **Tims Ford Lake** - Located about 80 miles south of Nashville, Tims Ford Lake is a popular destination for fishing and water sports. With over 10,000 acres of water, the lake is surrounded by rolling hills and scenic vistas. Visitors can explore the lake's many coves and islands, or relax on one of the many sandy beaches.

- **Dale Hollow Lake** - Located about 115 miles northeast of Nashville, Dale Hollow Lake is a hidden gem in the heart of the Cumberland Mountains. The lake is known for its clear blue waters and is a popular destination for fishing and boating. Visitors can explore the lake's many coves and inlets, or take a scenic drive along the shoreline.

9

Bring the Kids

Family Activities

There are countless family-friendly activities to choose from, whether you're exploring the city or venturing out to the surrounding areas. From visiting the Nashville Zoo and the Adventure Science Center to going on a riverboat cruise, a hike to see a waterfall, or checking out the famous Country Music Hall of Fame, Nashville is a great destination for families looking to make wonderful memories.

Additionally, Nashville's breweries and wineries are not just for grown-ups! They welcome families with open arms, offering a fun and relaxed environment for everyone. From outdoor seating and games to kid-friendly activities, there's something to keep everyone entertained.

And when it comes to hiking in the surrounding areas, families can embark on exciting adventures together, exploring the scenic trails surrounded by the lush beauty of Tennessee nature.

Here are a few more ideas for family activities:

- **Adventure Science Center** - This hands-on science museum is perfect for curious kids of all ages. From space exploration to many fields of science and technology, to the human body, there's something to learn and discover for everyone. From thrilling planetarium shows to engaging exhibits, the center sparks curiosity and inspires a love for scientific exploration in a fun and immersive way.

- **Nashville Zoo** - Home to over 2,700 animals, the Nashville Zoo is a great place to check out for animal-loving families. With exhibits featuring a variety of animals and exhibits from giraffes to kangaroos, plus a petting zoo and a playground, it's a full day of fun.

- **The Elephant Sanctuary** - If you went to the zoo and were wondering where the elephants are, they've retired and moved a little over an hour south! This place is a safe and peaceful haven for these gentle retirees, providing them with a natural environment to freely roam and socialize. With a focus on their well-being, the sanctuary offers specialized diets, enriching activities, and attentive veterinary care. Visitors can join educational programs and tours to learn about elephant conservation and support the sanctuary's mission of advocating for the welfare and protection of these majestic creatures.

- **Tennessee Safari Park** - About 2.5 hours west of Nashville, you can drive through the park in your own vehicle, and get up close and personal with a variety of exotic animals. Feed them right from your car window and watch as they roam freely in their natural habitats. It's a thrilling safari experience that will leave you with unforgettable memories of your encounter with these incredible creatures.

- **Cheekwood Estate & Gardens** - This historic mansion-turned-art-museum boasts 55 acres of gardens, sculptures, and art exhibitions. There's also a treehouse and a train for kids to enjoy.

- **Country Music Hall of Fame and Museum** - Music-loving families will enjoy exploring the history of country music and seeing artifacts from famous artists like Johnny Cash and Dolly Parton.

- **Nashville Children's Theatre** - This professional theater company offers productions for kids of all ages. From classic fairy tales to new plays, there's always something exciting happening on stage.

- **Lane Motor Museum** - Car enthusiasts of all ages will love this unique museum, which features over 500 cars from around the world. It's the perfect place to learn about the history and mechanics of cars.

- **Frist Art Museum** - This art museum offers hands-on activities for kids and family-friendly exhibitions. From contemporary art to classic paintings, there's something to inspire everyone's creativity.

- **Bicentennial Capitol Mall State Park** - This park offers a great view of the state capitol building and plenty of space for running, playing, and exploring. There's also a splash pad and a large map of Tennessee to climb on.

- **Nashville Shores** - Beat the summer heat at this water park on Percy Priest Lake. With water slides, wave pools, and lazy rivers, it's a great way to spend a day on the water.

Parks

Nashville's parks are like hidden gems waiting to be discovered, offering a perfect escape from the hustle and bustle of the city. With picturesque landscapes, greenways, playgrounds, picnic spots, and even music events, these parks are perfect for leisurely strolls, family outings, or simply enjoying a sunny day with friends.

- **Cumberland Park** - Located near the riverfront, Cumberland Park has a variety of play structures and features, including a splash pad and a climbing wall. The park also has picnic areas and beautiful views of the Cumberland River.

- **Dragon Park** - Located in the heart of the West End, Dragon Park is a whimsical park that features a large dragon sculpture as the centerpiece. Kids can climb on the dragon, play on the playground equipment, and enjoy the green space.

- **Sevier Park** - Sevier Park in the 12South neighborhood features a large playground area, splash pad, and plenty of space to run around. The park also has tennis and basketball courts, picnic areas, and a community center.

- **Centennial Park** - Centennial Park is a large, beautiful park located in the heart of Nashville. Kids will love playing on the playground equipment, exploring the gardens, and seeing the iconic Parthenon replica.

- **McCabe Park** - Located in West Nashville, McCabe Park has a large playground area, a skate park, and plenty of green space for kids to run around. The park also has picnic areas and tennis and basketball courts.

- **Shelby Bottoms Nature Center and Greenway** - The Shelby Bottoms Nature Center and Greenway is a great place for families to explore nature. The park has a nature center with interactive exhibits, as well as hiking and biking trails, a playground area, and beautiful views of the Cumberland River.

- **Bicentennial Capitol Mall State Park** - Bicentennial Capitol Mall State Park is a unique park that features historical exhibits, a beautiful fountain, and plenty of space for kids to run around. The park also has a playground area and beautiful views of the State Capitol building.

10

Arts and Theater

Broadway Musicals

Ahh, the magic of Broadway! Not to be confused with *downtown's* Broadway, the Tennessee Performing Arts Center, or TPAC for short, is a vibrant hub for all things theatrical in Nashville. The Broadway productions that come through here are nothing short of spectacular, transporting audiences to a world of song, dance, and drama that is unmatched. From the classics like Phantom of the Opera and Les Misérables to the latest hits like Hamilton and Dear Evan Hansen, TPAC brings the best of the Great White Way to Music City. The costumes, the sets, the lighting, the performances...everything comes together to create an unforgettable experience that will leave you humming show tunes for days, or forever if you're like me. So grab a ticket, settle into your seat, and let the magic of Broadway take you away at TPAC.

Museums

Nashville is a city that knows how to celebrate its rich history, and one of the best ways to do that is by visiting its museums. The Country Music Hall of Fame and Museum is a must-visit for anyone who loves country music (or even those who don't). You'll get to see amazing artifacts from legends like Elvis, Johnny Cash, and Dolly Parton, and learn about the genre's roots and evolution.

Meanwhile, the Adventure Science Center is perfect for curious young minds. This interactive museum features exhibits that teach kids about everything from space exploration to electricity, all while letting them have hands-on fun.

You'll always find something new and exciting to discover. No matter what your interests are, Nashville's museums offer something for everyone to enjoy.

- **Country Music Hall of Fame and Museum** - This museum showcases the rich history of country music with interactive exhibits, rare recordings, and priceless artifacts from legendary performers. It's a must-visit for music lovers of all ages.

- **Johnny Cash Museum** - Dedicated to the Man in Black himself, this museum features exhibits on Cash's life and career, including stage costumes, instruments, and personal items.

- **Lane Motor Museum** - Car enthusiasts will love this unique museum featuring a collection of rare and vintage vehicles from around the world, including cars, motorcycles, and even a few flying cars.

- **Adventure Science Center** - This interactive science museum is a blast for kids and adults alike, with hands-on exhibits on topics ranging from space exploration to the human body.

- **Belle Meade Plantation** - This historic plantation offers tours of the 1853 mansion, as well as horseback riding, wine tastings, and other special events.

- **The Hermitage** - Home of President Andrew Jackson, this historic site offers tours of the mansion and grounds, as well as educational exhibits and special events.

- **Tennessee State Museum** - Explore the history of Tennessee at this museum featuring exhibits on Native American culture, the Civil War, and more.

- **The George Jones** - Honoring the life and legacy of country music icon George Jones, this museum features exhibits on Jones' life and career, including stage costumes, awards, and memorabilia.

Art Galleries

Nashville boasts a robust and diverse arts scene, and its art museums are no exception. From contemporary works to classic masterpieces, the art museums in Nashville have something for everyone. The Frist Art Museum, housed in a former post office, houses an impressive collection of rotating exhibits, featuring everything from modern art to ancient artifacts.

- **The Frist Art Museum** - This contemporary art museum features a wide range of exhibitions and programming, from contemporary art to photography to historical retrospectives.

- **The Rymer Gallery** - Located in the heart of downtown Nashville, the Rymer Gallery features work from both emerging and established artists in a variety of mediums, from painting to sculpture to photography.

- **The Red Arrow Gallery** - This gallery focuses on contemporary art, featuring both local and national artists in a variety of mediums. They also host regular events and exhibitions throughout the year.

- **The Tinney Contemporary** - Located in the historic Arcade building in downtown Nashville, the Tinney Contemporary features a range of contemporary art from local and national artists, including painting, sculpture, and photography.

- **The Arts Company** - This gallery features a range of contemporary and traditional art, including painting, sculpture, photography, and more. They also host regular exhibitions and events throughout the year.

- **The David Lusk Gallery** - With locations in both Memphis and Nashville, the David Lusk Gallery features work from both emerging and established artists in a range of mediums, from painting to sculpture to photography.

- **The Cumberland Gallery** - This contemporary art gallery features work from both emerging and established artists in a variety of mediums, including painting, sculpture, and mixed media.

- **The LeQuire Gallery** - This gallery features a range of contemporary and traditional art, with a focus on sculpture and three-dimensional works.

- **The Bennett Galleries** - With locations in both Knoxville and Nashville, the Bennett Galleries features a range of contemporary and traditional art from both local and national artists, including painting, sculpture, and more.

- **The Gallery at Avalon Island** - Located in East Nashville, the Gallery at Avalon Island features work from both emerging and established artists in a variety of mediums, including painting, sculpture, and mixed media.

11

Holidays

Christmas

The Christmas season in Nashville is simply magical. The city transforms into a winter wonderland with twinkling lights, festive decorations, and a joyous spirit in the air. From the massive Christmas tree at the heart of downtown to the charming neighborhoods adorned with wreaths and garlands, there's a festive vibe everywhere you turn.

And don't forget the music! Nashville's famous live music scene takes on a holiday twist, with carolers, Christmas concerts, and special performances adding to the merriment. Plus, there are plenty of holiday markets, ice-skating rinks, and seasonal treats like hot cocoa and gingerbread to indulge in. Whether you're a local or a visitor, the Christmas season in Nashville is a time of warmth and cheer.

- **Christmas at Gaylord Opryland Hotel** - This is an annual event where the Gaylord Opryland Resort is transformed into a winter wonderland. There are ice sculptures, snow tubing, ice skating, and an indoor garden filled with more than 3 million twinkling lights. Disclaimer on this one: As of Christmas of 2022, you are required to be a guest of the hotel to enjoy the indoor delights and festivities.

- **Cheekwood Estate & Gardens Holiday Lights** - Every year, these beautiful botanical gardens transforms into a magical wonderland with over 1 million twinkling lights, beautiful Christmas trees, and live reindeer.

- **Nashville Christmas Parade** - This parade is a beloved Nashville tradition that takes place in early December. It features floats, marching bands, and, of course, Santa Claus himself.

- **Drive-Through Light Displays** - There are several drive-through light displays in Nashville during the Christmas season, including the Dancing Lights of Christmas at the Wilson County Fairgrounds and the Holiday Lights at the Historic Fontanel Mansion.

- **Dickens of a Christmas** - This annual festival in historic downtown Franklin features costumed characters, horse-drawn carriage rides, and over 200 vendors selling unique gifts and crafts.

- **Ice Skating at Ascend Amphitheater** - Ascend Amphitheater is transformed into a winter wonderland during the Christmas season, complete with an outdoor ice skating rink.

- **Nashville Symphony's Handel's Messiah** - The Nashville Symphony performs Handel's Messiah every year during the Christmas season, a beautiful and festive way to celebrate the holidays.

- **The Ryman Auditorium's Christmas at the Ryman** - The Ryman Auditorium, the famous former home of the Grand Ole Opry, hosts a variety of Christmas-themed shows throughout the holiday season.

- **Holiday Markets** - Nashville has several holiday markets where you can shop for unique gifts and crafts, including the Porter Flea Holiday Market and the Made South Holiday Market.

- **Visit Santa Claus** - There are several places to visit Santa in Nashville during the Christmas season, including the Gaylord

Opryland Resort, the Nashville Zoo, and the Bass Pro Shop in Opry Mills Mall.

Christmas Pop-Up Bars

Though they tend to change every year with surprise ones being added each Christmas season, here is a list of past Christmas themed pop-up bars we've had in the past:

- **Miracle at Hidden Bar**: This pop-up bar was known for its over-the-top holiday decorations and festive drinks. From the giant Christmas tree to the themed cocktails, visitors were transported to a winter wonderland.

- **Snow Globe at Nightscape**: Ever wondered what it was like to hang out inside a snow globe? Me neither. But here you can realize the experience you never knew you needed in an immersive setting featuring walls adorned with 360-degree projection mapping.

- **Reindeer Games**: This pop-up bar took inspiration from classic holiday movies and games. Visitors could sip on cocktails like "Frosty's Magic Hat" and play games like "Pin the Nose on Rudolph."

- **Sippin' Santa**: This tropical-themed pop-up bar put a festive spin on tiki drinks with holiday-themed cocktails like the "Rudolph Shoots the Curl." The bright, colorful décor was a welcome escape from the cold winter weather.

- **The Grinch's Grotto**: This pop-up bar took inspiration from the classic Dr. Seuss book and movie, with green décor and Grinch-themed cocktails. Visitors could even take a photo with the Grinch himself!

Fourth of July

Ask any local, and they will tell you Nashville's fireworks display has NYC beat, but we may be a bit biased. Either way, Nashville's Fourth of July fireworks show is widely regarded as one of the best in the nation. The display is known for its stunning pyrotechnic choreography, set against the backdrop of the city's iconic skyline.

The fireworks are launched from the Cumberland River and set to the tune of a live orchestral performance, creating a truly magical and unforgettable experience. It's a show that truly captures the spirit and pride of Nashville and one that thousands look forward to every year.

The energy and excitement in the air in Nashville on the 4th is palpable, as locals and visitors alike come together to celebrate Independence Day. As the sun sets, the city prepares for the main event: the fireworks display.

- **Ascend Amphitheater** - Located downtown, the amphitheater provides a stunning view of the fireworks along the Cumberland River. With live music and food vendors, it's the perfect spot for a night out with friends or family.

- **The Nashville skyline** - Find a rooftop bar or restaurant with a view of the city skyline, and you'll have an unbeatable view of the fireworks. It's a romantic and classy way to celebrate the Fourth of July.

- **Riverfront Park** - This is one of the most popular spots to watch the fireworks in Nashville. Located right on the riverfront, you can catch the fireworks show over the Cumberland River. Get there early to secure a good spot.

- **Cumberland Park** - Cumberland Park offers an up-close and personal view of the fireworks. You can also enjoy the playground, splash pad, and other outdoor activities before the fireworks show.

- **Nashville Shores** - Enjoy a day of fun at the water park and stay for the fireworks show at night. This is a great option for families who want to make a whole day out of the Fourth of July.

- **The General Jackson Showboat** - The showboat offers a unique way to watch the fireworks. You can enjoy a dinner cruise on the Cumberland River and watch the fireworks from the boat.

- **Towering city parking garages** - Grab your spot early atop a parking garage and enjoy an uninterrupted view of the skyline and the dazzling pyrotechnics display.

- **John Seigenthaler Pedestrian Bridge** - For a picture-perfect vantage point, head to the pedestrian bridge, which spans the Cumberland River between East Nashville and Downtown with great views of all three. The view from here is absolutely breathtaking as the fireworks reflect off of the river, but beware - it's also a popular spot, so be sure to arrive early to claim your turf.

- **The east bank of the river at East Park** - Get away from the bustling downtown and catch the fireworks with the stunning Nashville skyline as your backdrop from this viewpoint. Before the show, swing by the annual Hot Chicken Festival to indulge in Nashville's unique, fiery favorite. For an equally great view,

Cumberland Park on South First Street is another excellent option on the East Side.

12

Conclusion

With the wide variety of happenings in the Nashville area, it won't matter if you're a first-time visitor or a seasoned local – there's absolutely something for everyone, from the vibrant nightlife scene to the serene lakes and waterfalls. With this guide in hand, my hope is that you'll discover new and exciting ways to experience Nashville, create memories that will last a lifetime, and come back for more.

Nashville is a city that truly has it all, doesn't it? There aren't many places where you can hike to see a 100-foot waterfall, enjoy a world-class brunch, relax at a picturesque winery, and catch a Taylor Swift show all in one day. From the best food around to live music at every turn, incredible museums, and stunning parks, it's a place where you can't possibly experience everything in just one trip.

You could spend months exploring the different neighborhoods and still discover something new every day. Nashville's unique blend of Southern hospitality and big-city energy is infectious, and it's easy to see why so many people fall in love with the city after just one visit. So if you're planning a trip to Music City, get ready to be swept off your feet and take in as much as you can, because you'll most definitely be back for more.

Thank you so much for joining me, and I hope to see y'all around!

About the Author

Sarah is raising two boys and two dogs with her very attractive husband in the Nashville area and also sells real estate. In her hypothetical free time, she enjoys sitting down.

Printed in Great Britain
by Amazon